Energy and Matter in Ecosystems

Reader

ISBN: 978-1-68380-542-7

Energy and Matter in Ecosystems

Table of Contents

Chapter 1	**Producers, Consumers, and Decomposers** ...	1
Chapter 2	**Living Things Use Energy**	11
Chapter 3	**What Plants Need**	15
Chapter 4	**Energy Relationships Among Organisms** ...	23
Chapter 5	**Ecosystems**	29
Chapter 6	**Food Chains and Food Webs**	35
Chapter 7	**Rain Forest Ecosystem Field Diary**	41
Chapter 8	**Changes in Ecosystems**	47
Glossary	....	53

Producers, Consumers, and Decomposers

Some scientists suggest that there are almost nine million different kinds of living things, or **organisms**, on Earth. But wait! How do you know if something is living? Ask yourself the following questions:

Does it need food? Living things cannot survive without energy they get from food. Some living things make their own food. Some get food from other living things.

Big Question

Where do organisms get the energy they need for living?

Vocabulary

organism, n. a single living thing

Does it grow? All living things grow and change throughout their lives. Even the mighty elephant begins life as a tiny organism.

Does it reproduce? Living things reproduce to make offspring, more of their species.

Is it made of cells? A cell is the smallest living part of an organism. Some organisms are made of only one cell that can do everything needed to stay alive. Most living things, such as plants and animals, are made of more than one cell. You can see living cells by using a microscope.

What makes the sea cucumber alive while the rock is not?

Producers

What Is a Producer?

When you get hungry, you must get chemical energy from the food you eat. Imagine being able to make your own food without even moving. A **producer** is a

living thing that makes its own food. Plants, algae, and some one-celled organisms are producers. Every producer, no matter how large or small, makes its own food. It transforms one kind of energy into the chemical energy it needs to live.

Most producers need sunlight, water, and air to survive. Why? Because these are the things producers such as plants transform into stored energy in food.

Sunlight is a form of energy. Producers such as plants make food using sunlight.

How Do Producers Make Food?

Have you ever noticed that most plants are green? This is because their leaves and stems contain a chemical called *chlorophyll*. To make food, a plant needs chlorophyll, sunlight, water, and carbon dioxide gas from air.

The producer absorbs sunlight to make food. The type of food producers make is a kind of sugar called *glucose*. Producers can use the glucose right away as food or store the glucose for later. In the process of making glucose, the producer releases oxygen back into the air.

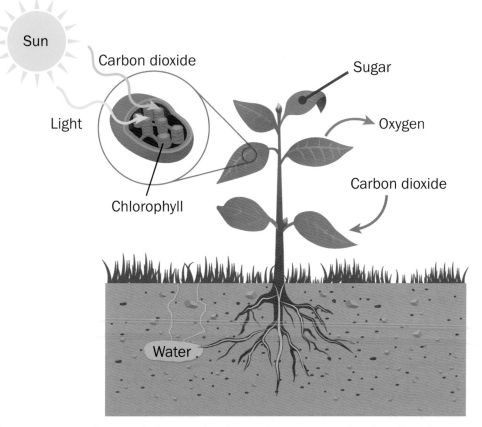

Plants use energy from sunlight to make glucose from water and carbon dioxide. Plants can use the sugar right away or store it for later use.

Consumers

What Is a Consumer?

Unlike producers that make their own food, at lunchtime you go to the cafeteria to eat. How do other living things get their food? **Consumers** are living things that get energy from consuming, or eating, other living things. Consumers cannot make their own food like producers do.

Are you a producer or a consumer? Do you make your food through the process plants use? No, you get it from other living things.

The pictures show two organisms commonly found in pond water. A green alga is shown at the top. It is a producer. You can tell it contains chlorophyll because of the green color. An amoeba is shown in the bottom picture. Amoebas are consumers that move around in water and absorb the food they consume.

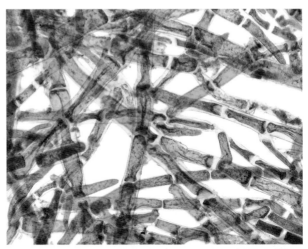

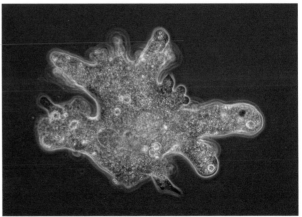

How Do Consumers Get Food?

Some consumers eat producers. Some consumers eat other consumers. Consumers such as barnacles and oysters remain in one place and take in food from the surrounding water. Many consumers move from place to place in different ways. Some move with legs, the way people do. Others crawl, fly, or swim. Compare the structures of the stingray, sea star, and snake. How does each of these animals move to get its food?

Some consumers, such as the barnacles attached to a whale, do not move as adults. They anchor themselves to some other object and strain food out of the water.

Stingrays swim through water and along the sea floor to find their food.

Sea stars swim or walk on the sea floor to catch their food.

Snakes slither and strike to catch their food.

Barnacles often attach themselves to things that move, such as this whale's tail.

Scavengers and Decomposers

What Are Scavengers and Decomposers?

All organisms produce waste throughout their lifetimes and eventually die and are broken down. If these materials were not broken down, they would pile up and bury us!

Many times, the first step to breaking these materials down falls to the scavengers. **Scavengers** are animals that feed on dead plant and animal material. Scavengers tend to live at the bottom of ecosystems, as this is where dead material tends to settle. In a forest, you can find scavengers such as earthworms and millipedes under pieces of bark or soil. Crab, shrimp, and lobster can be found at the bottom of bodies of water.

Vocabulary

scavenger, n. an animal that eats organisms that have already died

This hermit crab feeds on both live and dead plants and animals.

The dung beetle rolls dung into balls before storing and eating the dung.

Earthworms burrow through soil and eat dead plant matter.

Decomposers are organisms that complete the breakdown of organic materials. Decomposers remove any chemical energy from what remains and return the remaining matter to the soil. Some decomposers that return matter from other living things to the soil are fungi and bacteria.

Why do forests have so many mushrooms growing in them? Because mushrooms, types of fungi, have so much material to decompose in a forest. Almost all fungi are decomposers. Fungi

use energy from once-living materials to live and grow. Fungi also break the materials down into smaller pieces.

Bacteria are microscopic organisms that are found everywhere. You have bacteria inside and all over the outside of your body. Many bacteria help keep you healthy. There are also bacteria that are harmful to many things. Bacteria are also decomposers that extract the last little bits of nutrients and energy out of once-living material.

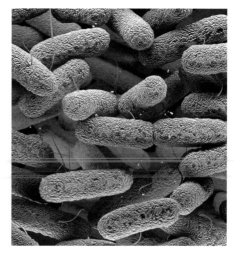

Bacteria are too small to be seen without a microscope.

Why Do Living Things Need Food?

Think about all the activities you do every day. You need energy to do them. Going to school, playing sports, and reading a book all take chemical energy. Remember that energy is the ability to cause a change. Chemical energy is required for the processes in your body that keep you alive. Living things need energy for keeping warm, moving, repairing damage, and growing. Where do you get energy to do these things? From the food you eat!

Living Things Need Chemical Energy to Move

Organisms need chemical energy to move and grow. This means that they need food in one form or another. Animals get their food from plants or other animals. One way they use that energy is in moving around to find more food. Or in moving to escape being food for something else!

Lions need chemical energy to move. They get that chemical energy by eating other animals. The energy they gain then helps them move to find more food. Wildebeests need chemical energy to power their escape!

Living Things Need Chemical Energy to Keep Warm

Most organisms cannot survive if their bodies become too hot or too cold. For example, the average internal temperature of a human body is 98.6 degrees Fahrenheit (°F). The polar bear's internal body temperature is about 98.6 °F, as well. In the polar bear's cold environment, it must use a lot of energy from food to maintain that internal body warmth.

Even animals such as turtles and frogs, which don't maintain a constant body temperature, need to be warm enough to live. They use energy to move into the sun to get some of their warmth.

The polar bear's thick fur keeps its it from losing internal body heat to the cold, outside air.

Turtles can warm their body using energy from the sun. They do not need to eat as much food as warm-blooded animals, but they still use food to help stay warm.

Living Things Need Chemical Energy to Repair Damage

If you get a scratch, in time it heals and goes away. Your body repairs the damage. Living things need chemical energy to repair damage to their bodies. The damage may be something you can see, such as a lizard that has a broken tail. Or the damage may be something you cannot see. Sometimes parts inside of organisms, such as bones and organs, become harmed by injury or illness. Cells use chemical energy to make new, healthy tissue in the healing process.

Living Things Need Chemical Energy to Grow and Reproduce

Plants and animals grow when their bodies produce new cells and tissues. They need energy for the growth process. Some organisms grow only for a short period of time, just after they are born. Other organisms, such the bristlecone pine tree, grow throughout their entire lives. Bacteria almost never grow large enough to be seen by the unaided eye. However, they must use energy to make more bacteria.

This lizard lost its tail. It is using energy to repair itself and grow a new tail.

Living Things Use Energy

What happens to food after you chew and swallow it? It is broken down into nutrients that your body can take in for nutrition. Food is broken down into carbohydrates, protein, fat, vitamins, and minerals. The materials called carbohydrates become **sugars**, from which the body gets energy. Sugars exist in many chemical forms, such as glucose, sucrose, and fructose. The word *carbohydrates* contains parts of the words *carbon* and *hydrogen*. Sugars contain atoms of carbon and hydrogen, but they also contain oxygen.

Big Question

How do organisms use energy that originally comes from the sun?

Vocabulary

sugar, n. a carbohydrate that living things break down to get energy

Think about the sugar people use when baking. It is sucrose. Sucrose comes from sugarcane, a plant. But as tasty as sucrose is, an even more important sugar, glucose, sustains most life on Earth—and it is made using energy from the sun.

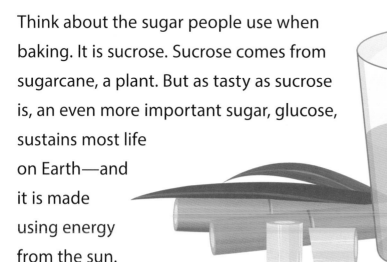

Sugarcane is a plant that uses sunlight to make sugar. People crush the sugarcane to get its juice. The juice is then heated until the water in it evaporates. A sugary syrup remains.

Energy from the Sun

Look around, and notice every living thing you can see that uses food—chemical energy—as energy. Even plants have to use chemical energy to live.

Where does the chemical energy for life come from? You know that it comes from sunlight. Remember that energy can be transformed from one form to another. Sunlight strikes the leaves of plants, and that light energy is transformed into the energy of the sugar **glucose**—the chemical energy of life.

Making and Storing Energy

Plants are producers that make food using the process of **photosynthesis**. Photosynthesis occurs when plants combine carbon dioxide and water with energy from sunlight to make glucose and oxygen.

| Carbon Dioxide | + | Water | + | Sunlight | → | Glucose | + | Oxygen |

The transformation of sunlight into the chemical energy of glucose takes place most often in the leaves of plants. Leaves take in sunlight and use its energy in a process that makes chemical energy. Some of this energy is used by producers to live. The rest of the energy is stored in the producer, often as starch.

Moving Stored Energy Among Organisms

All of the energy of life starts with the sun and from the glucose that is made by producers. Other organisms in addition to plants are producers too, such as algae. Producers use the chemical energy in glucose to live. But plants and other producers get eaten too—often by you! You consume plants and thus are a consumer.

Transferring Stored Energy

Consumers get glucose when they eat producers or organisms that have eaten producers. A plant, such as grass, makes chemical energy from sunlight. A cow eats grass and uses the energy to grow. We eat beef and get some of the energy we need to grow. Energy stored by the plant is passed from organism to organism.

Releasing and Using Stored Energy

Inside living cells, oxygen and glucose undergo a chemical reaction. The process releases energy and carbon dioxide. The carbon dioxide is carried away from cells as a waste product. The energy released is used by the cells for different things. The cells can grow. They can repair damage. They can work together to move the organism. Sometimes they can help produce heat to keep the living thing warm.

Metabolism Releases Energy

The chemical energy of glucose, once it is released in the cell, can be used to power thousands of chemical reactions. Chemical reactions are always happening inside living things. This ongoing energy use is known as **metabolism**.

Different living things use energy to support their life processes at different rates. You may have heard the phrase, "That person has a great metabolism." It means that his or her body breaks down sugars and releases energy in a way that keeps that person from gaining excess weight.

The hummingbird has the fastest metabolism of all animals, about 100 times faster than that of an elephant! Tiny hummingbirds fly from flower to flower all day collecting nectar for food. They need to consume more than twice their body weight of food every day to stay alive. Their bodies store just enough energy to make it through one night to the next day.

Hummingbirds move their wings so fast that they look blurry to our vision. This requires the hummingbird's body to metabolize sugar very quickly.

In contrast, many snakes can survive for over a year without eating. These animals use very little chemical energy to keep their bodies warm, and their metabolisms are very slow.

What Plants Need

Imagine that you measure the weight of a seed. Then you measure the weight of a pot with soil in it. You put the seed in the pot and wait for it to grow. Every day for a month, you water the plant. You measure the weight of the water, too.

Big Question

Where do plants get the materials they need for growth?

Imagine how the plant will change. Finally, you remove the plant from the pot and weigh it. It has gained one pound! But the weight of the pot and soil has hardly changed. How did the plant gain so much material if it did not consume the soil? A scientist named Jan van Helmont wondered the same thing. Let's find out what happened!

As a plant grows larger, it does not consume the soil in which it grows. Where does the plant's new weight come from?

Plants Need Sunlight

You have likely never seen grass thickly carpeting a forest floor. Though some plants can survive in shadier places, all plants need sunlight to live. This is why plants do not grow under rocks and why many plants would struggle to survive in heavy shade beneath trees.

Plants use sunlight to make glucose, their food. Sunlight is not a food ingredient, however. It is the energy source plants use to start the chemical reaction to make glucose. Recall that during the process of photosynthesis, plants use water and carbon dioxide to make glucose and oxygen. If a plant does not absorb enough sunlight, it cannot complete the chemical process to make sugar. With too little sugar, the plant does not grow well.

A square of cardboard was placed over the grass and left this shape. The grass that was shaded from the sun is now not as healthy as the surrounding grass.

Getting Sunlight

Most people think of plants as motionless, but plants do subtly move on their own. Plants must have sunlight to survive, so they can change positions to help them absorb the most sunlight possible.

You may have seen a plant near a window bending toward the sun. The cells on the side of the stem that are not getting sunlight stretch out. This makes the plant stem bend so that more of the plants leaves are positioned in direct sunlight.

A few types of plants that live in water do not have stems. Instead, they grow large leaves that float on top of the water. Keeping their leaves above the surface of the water helps them to gather as much sunlight as they can.

What will happen if this plant's pot is rotated so that the stems are leaning away from the window?

Plants Need Water

How do plants take in the water that they need to live? Most plants soak up water from soil with their roots. The roots of some plants can be close to the surface. This way, they can soak up rainwater quickly in dry environments. Other roots grow deep into the earth. Tree roots have been found 400 feet (122 meters) below ground, inside of a cave. Roots grow as far as they can to get water for the plant.

Water absorbed by roots travels upward into the stem. From the stem, it moves into the leaves. In the leaves, water is one of the materials for photosynthesis.

Notice the many tiny roots branching off from the main roots. Roots spread out to find water in the soil.

Plants also sometimes release water. On a sunny day, put a plastic bag over a plant. Before long, tiny water droplets will collect in the bag. The process by which water vapor is released by plants is called **transpiration**.

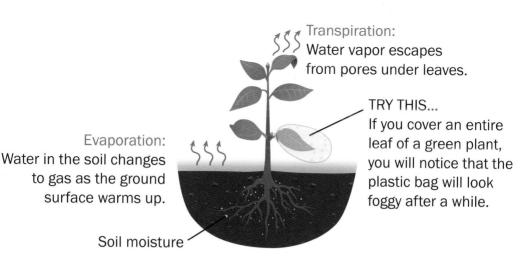

Transpiration:
Water vapor escapes
from pores under leaves.

TRY THIS...
If you cover an entire
leaf of a green plant,
you will notice that the
plastic bag will look
foggy after a while.

Evaporation:
Water in the soil changes
to gas as the ground
surface warms up.

Soil moisture

Plants Need Air

Leaves have many tiny, microscopic holes. These holes open to let air in and out. Importantly, plants take in carbon dioxide through these small openings. They release oxygen too.

Plants use the carbon dioxide to help them make food. Oxygen is one result of the process. When animals breathe in air, they use the oxygen. They breathe out carbon dioxide as waste. When plants let air into their leaves, they use the carbon dioxide. They release oxygen as waste.

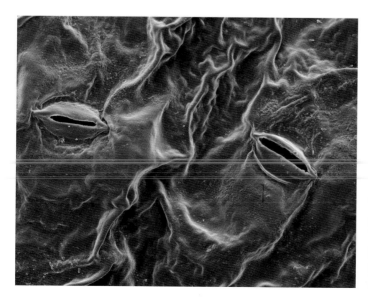

The microscopic pores in plants are called *stomata*. They take in carbon dioxide from the air to enable the plant to make food. They also let out oxygen.

Investigating the Weight of Plants

Jan van Helmont, a Dutch scientist, did a famous plant investigation almost 400 years ago. He measured the weight of a plant and the weight of the soil it grew in. His experiments showed that the plant weighed a lot more after growing for several years but that the weight of the soil remained the same.

What did this mean? Plants do not increase in weight by taking in the soil. He explained that plants increase in weight from the matter they take in from air.

Do Plants Need Soil?

Plants do not need soil to live. They use nutrients from the soil that dissolve in water, but they do not absorb the soil. Some farmers grow plants without soil. This is called

hydroponics. The word part *hydro* means water. In this kind of farming, plants grow with only sunlight and water with added nutrients.

In this hydroponic tank, you can see the plants' roots.

Plants Are Important to All Life on Earth

Plants are the basis for all animals' food. Think about the plants you have used today. If you ate fruits or vegetables, you used plants. Every food you eat either came from a plant or from something that ate plants.

Plants provide materials. A desk is made of wood. So are paper and pencils. You might even be wearing plants! Cotton is a type of plant that many clothes are made of.

This is what a cotton plant looks like. What properties can you observe that may make cotton a good plant to use for clothing?

Plants provide oxygen. Plants release oxygen as waste. Almost every other living thing on Earth needs oxygen to live. Plants on land release oxygen into the air. Plants that grow in water release oxygen into the water. Fish take in the oxygen through their gills. They, too, rely on oxygen to live.

If you look closely at this picture, you can see tiny bubbles on the water plant. These bubbles are oxygen.

Plants prevent erosion. Plants hold soil down with their roots. This keeps soil from blowing away. It also keeps it from washing away. The roots of plants growing on sand dunes help anchor the dunes in place. Without sand dunes, coastal areas could become flooded.

Plants provide medicine. People get medicine from some kinds of plants. Almost one-fourth of all medicines come from plants. If you have ever had a sore throat, you may have used a cough drop that contained lemon and mint. Some pain medicines come from a type of tree bark. Many ingredients in vitamins come from plants.

The roots of plants help prevent erosion of sand and soil.

The bark of a type of willow tree is the source of the chemical used in aspirin.

Energy Relationships Among Organisms

Plants make the sugar glucose through photosynthesis. Plants need glucose to survive. Animals need glucose, too. They must consume food to get this energy. For survival, animals depend on other living things, such as plants and other animals.

Big Question

Where do different organisms get their energy?

Once plants make chemical energy, that energy flows through all the animals that eat the plants and other animals in a given area. This is called energy flow. Energy flows from producers (plants) to the consumers that eat plants, to the consumers that eat animals.

Energy passes from the sun to plants, to animals, and then to other animals. We can trace energy flow in any environment.

The gopher tortoise uses energy from the sun in two ways. It warms itself in sunlight. And it eats the cactus, which contains glucose that the cactus produced using the sun's energy.

Example: Matter and Energy Flow in a Coral Reef

1. Larger algae and tiny algae too small to be seen without a microscope are producers that use sunlight to make food.

2. Coral filters algae from the water. Small fish and crustaceans, such as shrimp, also eat the algae and seaweed to get energy. These organisms that eat only producers are called **herbivores**.

3. Bigger fish eat smaller fish to get energy. Animals that eat other animals are known as **carnivores**.

4. Energy gets to the largest fish and into deeper, dark parts of the ocean by passing through other living things first.

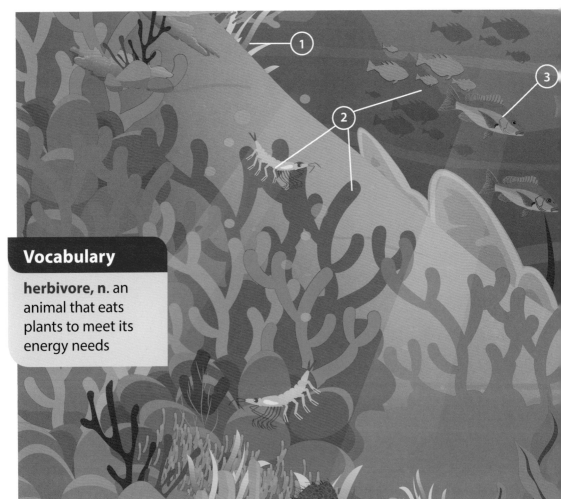

Vocabulary

herbivore, n. an animal that eats plants to meet its energy needs

5. Scavengers such as crabs get energy from eating dead algae and fish.

6. Bacteria decompose the remaining material and return the last of the matter back to the ecosystem environment.

7. Matter, as well as energy, flows through the environment. For example, as algae use sunlight to make food, they release oxygen into the water. The fish take in oxygen from the water through their gills.

Vocabulary

carnivore, n. an animal that eats other animals to meet its energy needs

Example: Matter and Energy Flow in a River

1. Algae and water plants use energy from the sun to make food.

2. Small minnows eat algae and plants. Mussels ingest organic matter that is in the water.

3. Larger fish get energy from eating the minnows.

4. Crabs get energy from eating the mussels and small minnows. They may also eat any dead things they find.

5. Water birds get energy by eating small fish such as minnows.

6. Raccoons also get energy from eating fish and mussels. Raccoons also eat vegetation growing on the land nearby.

7. Like raccoons, people can eat animals from the river environment, but they also eat plants. Organisms that eat both plants and other animals are known as **omnivores**.

Vocabulary

omnivore, n. an animal that eats both plants and other animals to meet its energy needs

Example: Matter and Energy Flow in a Desert

1. Sagebrush, cacti, and other plants use sunlight, air, and scarce water to make glucose.

2. Jackrabbits and other rodents get energy from eating the leaves and flowers of the sagebrush and other plants.

3. Some lizards, such as the bearded dragon, are omnivores. They consume other animals, such as insects, as well as plants.

4. A brown snake gets energy from eating a lizard.

5. Coyotes primarily get energy from eating other animals, such as the snake or jackrabbit. When animal food sources are scarce, the coyote adopts omnivorous habits and resorts to plant material for food.

Ecosystems

An **ecosystem** includes all the living and nonliving things that interact in a given area. You can think of an ecosystem as a neighborhood of living things. So, how does the meaning of *ecosystem* differ from that of the words *environment* and *habitat*? An environment is one geographic area. Ecosystems also include a sense of the a flow of energy and matter.

Ecosystems vary widely in size. An ecosystem may be as large as a huge lake or as small as a moss-covered rock. Do you think this single tree is an example of an ecosystem? Yes! It is. There are other organisms that live their entire lives getting everything they need without ever leaving the tree.

This tree is also part of a much larger ecosystem, a Central American forest ecosystem. Some of these forests cover vast areas. But all the living and nonliving things compose this Central American forest ecosystem.

A scientist, Terry Erwin, wondered how many insects live in the ecosystem of just one tree. He found more than 1,200 different kinds of insects living there.

Big Question

What is an ecosystem, and what are some different types of ecosystems?

Vocabulary

ecosystem, n. all the living and nonliving things that interact in a given area

Ecosystems Contain Living Things

Ecosystems are made up of many kinds of organisms, including producers, consumers, and decomposers. These organisms depend on one another for food and energy. In an ecosystem, producers make energy from the sun. Consumers eat the producers, and some consumers eat other consumers. Finally, decomposers help break down matter and energy and return it to the earth. This helps new plants grow again.

A healthy ecosystem has many different types of living things in it. Most of those living things interact in some way and depend on one another, either directly or indirectly.

Agriculture changes a naturally occurring ecosystem into a human-developed ecosystem.

Ecosystems Contain Nonliving Things

The living things in an ecosystem also depend on the nonliving environment. Factors such as temperature, rainfall, fog, wind, and sunlight all affect the ecosystem.

Water

Every living thing needs water to survive. Most animals live in or near a pond, stream, river, or ocean. Even when water cannot be seen, living things have ways to find hidden sources. Animals can eat fruit or plants to get the water stored inside.

Plants use their roots to find water deep within the soil and to collect water quickly from the soil when it rains. Rainwater is an important part of many ecosystems. Think about a tropical rain forest. These places get a lot of rain, so a lot of plants can grow there. The rainwater also provides water to the animals. Now think about a desert ecosystem. Deserts do not get a lot of rain, yet they still support the organisms that live there. How is this possible?

Many plants and animals have adapted to the conditions in deserts. For example, the cactus is a plant that does not need a lot of constant water to grow. When it rains in the desert, some cacti soak up the rainwater and store it in their trunks for months or years, using it as a reserve supply to keep them hydrated until it rains again. Animals that live in deserts have learned to find ways to get water out of the cacti, such as by drilling holes into the trunks or drinking the water from their fruit.

This plump fruit that grows on a cactus contains water.

Sunlight and Soil

Sunlight and the types of sediment in soil are important nonliving parts of ecosystems. Producers need sunlight to make food. Getting more sunlight means producers can make more food. In turn, this allows them to provide more food and more homes to other organisms.

Different textures of soil may hold water or allow it to drain away more quickly. The type of soil affects the types of plants that can take root and survive in a place. Compare the soil where the plants in these two photos are growing. Which type of soil seems to support a greater variety of plant life?

Some plants, such as this vine, grow up trees to get high above the ground. The higher they climb, the more sunlight they can gather with their leaves.

Water drains through and evaporates out of sandy soil more quickly than it does soil that contains more organic material and clay.

Shelter

Living things need shelter to survive. They may depend on nonliving things such as rocks, burrows in the ground, or shells that their own bodies produce to make their home. Organisms may depend on other living things for shelter, such as a tree branch, a coral reef, or the mouth of an animal. In fact, your own body is an ecosystem that supports millions of other organisms. The human body contains many types of bacteria that are not only harmless, but also helpful to your health.

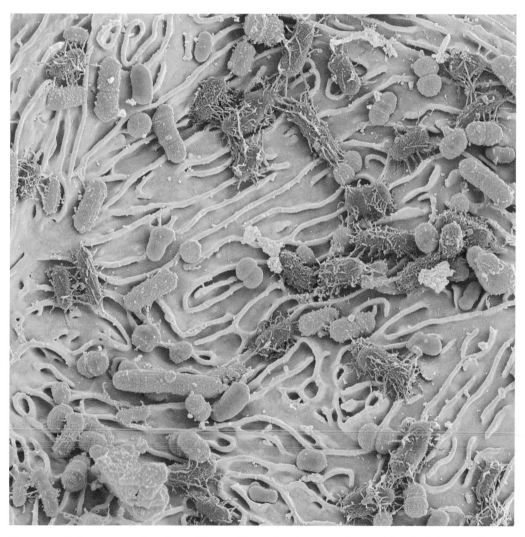

Your mouth is an ecosystem for millions of harmless bacteria. It provides shelter as well as moisture and food.

Ecosystems Vary Greatly

Ecosystems can be any size. They can span from the very small, such as a small pond, to the very large, such as miles and miles of deep ocean. The Great Barrier Reef, in eastern Australia, is an ecosystem that is 14,300 miles (23,000 kilometers) long. This is a large ecosystem. An aquarium is an example of an artificial ecosystem that is very small. An aquarium can be made with just one or two gallons of water. In the tank, a person can put everything a fish needs to survive.

Even a single drop of pond water can be an ecosystem. It can have everything necessary for tiny plankton to live their lives. The thing that large and small ecosystems have in common is that they both contain the things that are necessary for organisms to survive.

When you think of the word *ecosystem*, think of three things: a well-defined area, all the living things in it, and all the nonliving things that are a part of it.

This plant terrarium is a small ecosystem.

Food Chains and Food Webs

Organisms need energy to survive, grow, and reproduce. Producers make chemical energy from the sun by photosynthesis. Consumers get their energy from eating producers and other consumers. Decomposers get energy from dead material from producers and consumers. All living organisms are part of a **food chain**.

A food chain is a series of organisms listed in a way that shows which is a food source for another. It shows a flow of energy through an ecosystem. It is called a food chain because each organism serves as an important link for transferring energy and matter. If an eagle ate a mouse, the food chain could look like this:

Big Question

What are food chains and food webs?

Vocabulary

food chain, n. a series of organisms listed in a way that shows which is a food source for another

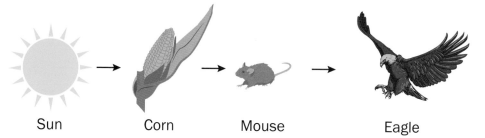

| Sun | Corn | Mouse | Eagle |

Energy passes from the sun into corn, a producer, which is consumed by a mouse. Then the mouse is consumed by an eagle.

The food chain for any organism begins with the producer, which gets energy from the sun. A producer then is food for a consumer. In this example, the first consumer is the mouse that eats the corn. The next-level consumer is the eagle that eats the mouse.

A Food Web Shows Related Food Chains

Within an ecosystem, consumers and decomposers can get food from several sources. So, ecosystems contain many food chains that connect in many ways. Sometimes the food chains overlap. For instance, a food chain could start with a producer, such as a corn plant. If the corn is eaten by more than one consumer, then it is part of multiple food chains, one for each consumer that eats the corn.

A **food web** is multiple connected food chains in an ecosystem. The arrows in the food web diagram point from the organism that is the food source toward the organism that eats each food. Animals that have no arrow pointing away from them are the top consumers. This means that there is nothing that eats them. The top consumers are usually found at the top of a food web, and they are often predators.

Food webs are a picture of energy flow in an ecosystem. There is no way to include all the energy relationships in an ecosystem in a single diagram, because there are too many!

Examine the food web on the next page. Find a food that more than one animal depends on. Locate an animal that eats several types of food. Which animals are top consumers in this food web?

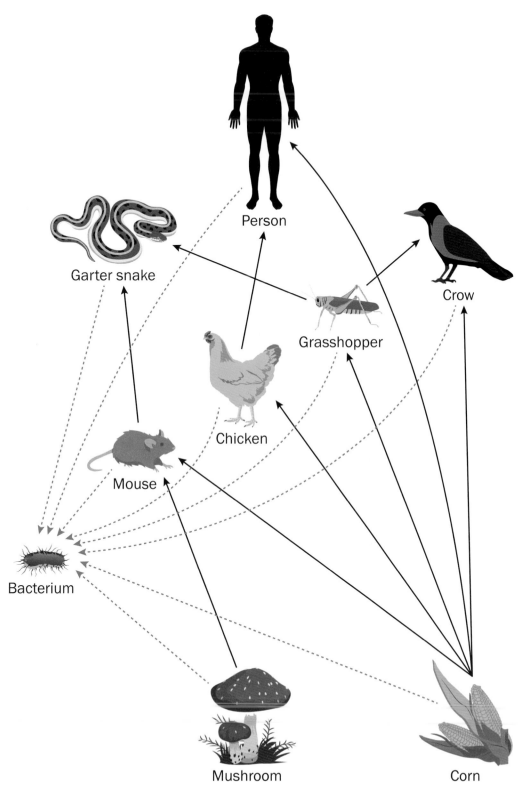

Person

Garter snake

Crow

Grasshopper

Chicken

Mouse

Bacterium

Mushroom

Corn

This food web shows living things in an ecosystem that depend on one another for food. Sometimes many organisms depend on the same type of food. Some organisms may get energy from eating several different types of food in the ecosystem.

Food Chains and Food Webs Show Matter and Energy Flow

Each food chain or web starts with the glucose and other chemicals in a producer. The producer must be eaten by a consumer to be part of a food chain. Look at the diagram below. The movement of the matter—and its stored chemical energy—can be traced by following the arrow from one organism in the chain to the next. Kelp are large brown algae that perform photosynthesis, so they are producers.

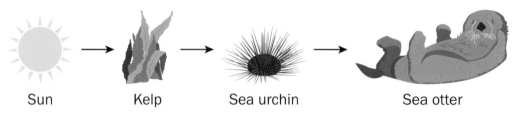

| Sun | Kelp | Sea urchin | Sea otter |

Energy from the sun passes to the kelp. Matter, in the form of glucose and other chemicals, passes from the kelp to the sea urchin. Food material, and the energy stored in it, passes from the sea urchin to the sea otter.

Energy in every common ecosystem can be traced back to the sun. Tracing the path of the arrows backward in a food chain or web will lead to the producer.

Look at the food web on the next page. This is a food web in a marine ecosystem. Phytoplankton are small photosynthetic organisms. They are producers. They make glucose using energy from sunlight.

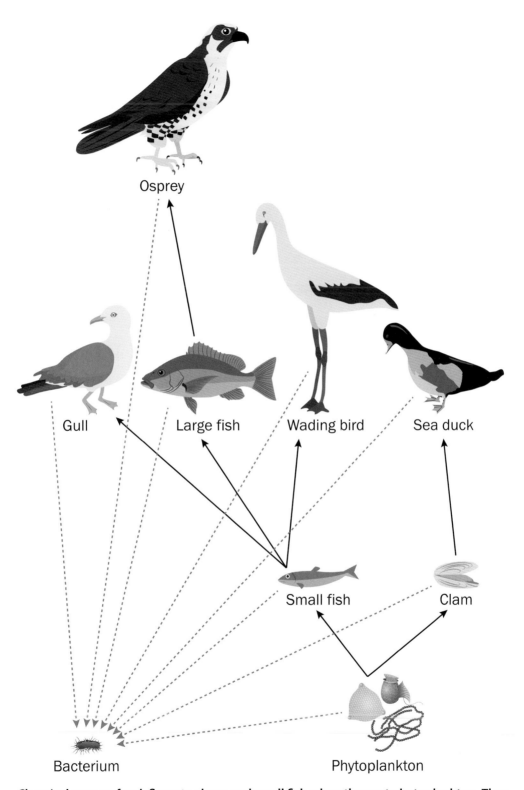

Osprey

Gull Large fish Wading bird Sea duck

Small fish Clam

Bacterium Phytoplankton

Chemical energy, food, flows to clams and small fish when they eat phytoplankton. Then matter flows to sea ducks when they eat clams. It flows to wading birds, gulls, and large fish when they eat smaller fish. Food material finally carries matter and energy to the osprey when the osprey, a top consumer, eats large fish.

Food Chains and Food Webs Explain Relationships

Food chains and food webs can help people understand relationships between living things in an ecosystem. For instance, if something causes there to be fewer otters in a kelp forest, a food chain or food web could help you predict the effect of fewer otters on other things in the ecosystem. A food web can help you see which organisms depend on which organisms for food and survival.

With fewer otters, there would likely be more sea urchins. This is because otters eat sea urchins. Without otters, sea urchins would not be eaten. This means more sea urchins would eat more kelp. As a result, the kelp forest would be smaller. Other animals besides sea urchins depend on kelp forests to live in and to get food. The smaller kelp forests would also affect these animals.

A kelp forest ecosystem is powered by the energy of sunlight. If the forest grew thick enough to block much of the sunlight, what else in the ecosystem might change?

Tuesday, 6:30 a.m.

A new day has dawned here in the Amazon rain forest. The sun is rising, but there are so many plants and trees that much of the sunlight does not shine through. A misty fog has rolled in, and it feels quite dark down here beneath the canopy!

Big Question

What goes on in a rain forest ecosystem?

The rain forest is a busy place, even this early in the morning. I am surrounded by the calls of birds and the buzz of insects. Some animals rustle in the nearby shrubs and plants. It is also very damp—the herbs and trees constantly fill the air with water vapor. On top of that, it rains nearly every day.

As I write this, I am sitting with my back against a tall mahogany tree. An orchid clings to its side. The orchid's roots do not actually reach the soil on the forest floor. Instead, they grab like fingers onto the tree's bark! As raindrops run down the tree's trunk, the orchid's roots soak it up.

wild orchid

Tuesday, 10:30 a.m.

The rain forest is awake! I hear macaws loudly calling to each other in the trees above me. They are communicating about where to find their morning meal. I have observed their bright blue feathers in the nearby banana trees. They love to eat fruit and seeds. I have even observed them eating the flowers of orchids!

Tuesday, 12:00 p.m.

After lunch, I decided to explore a dense patch of bamboo plants. I was quite surprised to encounter a monkey clinging to one of the stalks. It was chewing on a leaf. I have seen monkeys eating bananas and coconuts, but never bamboo.

I have noticed that monkeys are messy eaters! They drop bits of banana as they swing from branch to branch. Ants, one of the scavengers of the rain forest, benefit from this. I observed an army of them carrying one of the smaller pieces of dropped fruit back to the nest.

blue macaw

a monkey on a bamboo plant

Tuesday, 2:45 p.m.

As I continued through the dense forest, I heard a ruckus above me. I saw what looked at first to be a flying fox. It was large and furry, and it had wings! But after checking my field guide, I determined that it was a fruit bat. Fruit bats are one of the few species of bats that are active during the day. They eat fruit. This group was roosting and feeding in a coconut tree.

I approached the coconut tree carefully. Grasshoppers crawled up and down its trunk. A species of green tree frog sat nearby, camouflaged in the thick leaves of a small plant. Suddenly, it uncurled its long, sticky tongue and caught a grasshopper.

fruit bat

The green tree frog waits to catch its meal.

Tuesday, 4:00 p.m.

At this time of the day, the sun is high, and it is very hot. I decided to move deeper into the forest, where it is cooler. At one point, I came across a fallen log that was blocking the path. I used my walking stick to poke around in the soil under the log. The ground was covered in dead leaves and other plant material. Millipedes scurried away as I moved it aside. They seem to like eating the decaying material.

I was not surprised to find several earthworms slithering around under the log. Earthworms are decomposers. They love to eat the dead and decaying plant matter on the forest floor. When they eliminate waste, they return nutrients to the soil.

I also observed some brightly colored coral fungi on the decaying trunk. Coral fungi are decomposers, too.

earthworm

coral fungus

Tuesday, 7:00 p.m.

The sun was beginning to set, so I decided to make my way back to my campsite. Up ahead, I could see something coiled around a tree branch. As I got closer, I realized it was a green tree python! Pythons are very large snakes. They feed on birds, reptiles, and small mammals. They can sense the body heat of other animals, even in the dark! I have seen them on the hunt both at night and during the day. This one did not look like it had eaten recently. When night falls, it may slither down from the tree and go on the hunt for its next meal.

green tree python

Wednesday, 6:00 a.m.

Overnight, there was quite a bit of activity outside my tent! I could hear vampire bats screeching as they flew across the sky searching for prey. Like their name suggests, they drink the blood of other animals. They slit the skin of their prey with their teeth and then lap up the blood with their tongues!

When I emerged from my tent this morning, I found the remains of an animal beneath a nearby tree. I suspect that a leopard was hunting near the campsite overnight. Once they catch their prey, leopards climb a tree to eat it. The remains will eventually attract vultures. I have seen some perching in the tops of the trees already!

vampire bat

A leopard rests in trees during the day and hunts at night.

Changes in Ecosystems

Ecosystems are homes to varieties of living things and include all the factors that organisms need to live. All parts of an ecosystem are linked to and affect other parts. A change in one part of an ecosystem can affect other parts of that ecosystem. These changes can affect every living thing in the system. A change in an ecosystem that affects organisms is known as a **disruption**.

Some of the coral in the picture is healthy. Other coral is diseased and suffers from bleaching. Some type of disruption must have occurred.

Big Question

What happens when ecosystems are disrupted?

Vocabulary

disruption, n. a disturbance that interrupts a process

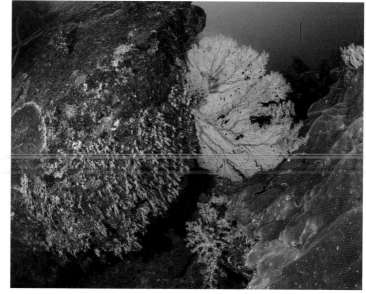

This ecosystem has had a disruption. Think about ways that the changes in the ecosystem may affect all living things in the system.

Natural Events Cause Ecosystem Disruptions

Ecosystem disruptions may happen for many reasons. Some disruptions have natural causes. However, humans cause many ecosystem disruptions, too. People can try to slow down or stop such changes. Sometimes the ecosystem can recover, but sometimes it is forever damaged.

Fire: Forest fires, or wildfires, are disruptive to the organisms that live in the places where they burn. Ecosystems that are disrupted by forest fires take many years to recover. Some forest fires have natural causes, such as lightning. In many ecosystems, fire is a part of a cycle that keeps the ecosystem healthy.

There are actually some benefits to fire. For example, a fire can burn dead brush and make room for new plants to grow. This can help an ecosystem flourish. Some types of pine trees only release their seeds when a fire heats their cones. The release of these seeds can help enhance an ecosystem, too.

After a fire, different types of trees and plants may grow in place of the ones that died. Some of the species that were in the ecosystem may return. These changes supply evidence that ecosystems are always changing and adapting to disruptions.

Fire has burned the trees and grass off this hill, but new plant life is already thriving.

Weather Events: As with lightning causing forest fires, weather events can cause a disruption of ecosystems. A drought is a long period where no rain or snow falls. Drought slows the growth of plants in an ecosystem. Any animal that eats those plants for energy will be affected by having less food. Long periods of extreme heat or cold also have an effect on the growth of organisms in an ecosystem.

Geologic Events: Many large-scale geologic events disrupt ecosystems. When a volcano erupts, it destroys the ecosystem in the immediate area and disrupts the ecosystem in a larger area. Earthquakes can cause tsunamis, large waves that cross the ocean. When a tsunami crashes into land, the size and force of the wave disrupt the ecosystem.

A volcanic eruption in 1980 blew the right side of Mount St. Helens apart. Almost forty years later, the area around the mountain has a healthy ecosystem.

Disease: Remember bacteria as a decomposer? Some of those bacteria can also become dangerous when they become a disease that infects an ecosystem. The coral on the first page of this chapter has a disease that causes the coral to die. Deer in some regions can suffer from chronic wasting disease, which destroys the deer's brain and leads to death.

Human Behaviors Cause Ecosystem Disruptions

Overfishing: Humans can disrupt the ocean ecosystem by overfishing. This means removing enough of one species of a water-dwelling organism that it harms that species' ability to continue. Let's look at how removing a species in a food web could affect the food web.

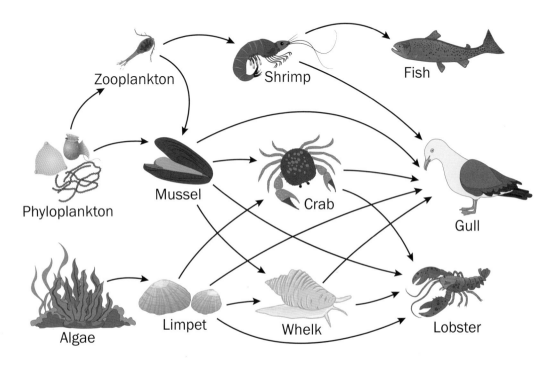

One chain in this web is phytoplankton → mussel → crab → gull. Now consider the effects if crab were overfished. The seagull would still get food from other sources. But what would happen to the mussels if more of them were surviving? There would then be more mussels. More mussels means they would need to eat more plankton. Soon there would be less plankton as the mussels eat more plankton. With less plankton, there is one less producer to add oxygen and energy to the ecosystem.

Deforestation: When people build houses, roads, or buildings, they often need to cut down trees to make room. Each tree can be home to many different types of living things. There may be insects, birds, squirrels, and even other plants depending on a tree to survive.

Humans have also cut down large areas of forest, such as in the Amazon basin, to create farmland on which to raise crops and livestock. It is estimated that at the rate humans are deforesting the rain forest, there will be no more rain forests on the planet in 100 years. Currently, humans have deforested twenty percent of all the forests on the planet.

Invasive Species: Invasive species can occur naturally, but frequently, humans bring them to an area. Because they developed in another area, invasive species can thrive because they may have no predators or competition for resources. Buckthorn trees were brought to the United States in the 1900s to be used as hedges. Buckthorn competes with native plants such as oak trees for nutrients, light, and moisture.

The dodo bird went extinct after humans started deforesting Mauritius, the island on which the dodo lived. Humans also brought invasive species, such as pigs and monkeys, that disrupted the dodo's ecosystem.

Water Pollution: Water is necessary to all life on Earth and to almost all ecosystems, but many human activities disrupt this part of many ecosystems. We use chemicals such as soaps and detergents that are harmful to the environment. Some can get into bodies of water and act as fertilizer. This causes some producers in the ecosystem to grow too much and ruin the delicate balance.

Another human activity that affects the water supply is our use of oil. People drill into Earth's crust under the oceans to get oil. When they do this, oil sometimes spills into water. Plants cannot take in matter to make food when they have oil on their leaves. Fish get oil in their gills, preventing them from getting oxygen. Birds cannot fly with oil in their feathers.

Some Disruptions Can Be Avoided

There is little humans can do to prevent natural ecosystem disruptions. We cannot stop an earthquake or volcano from happening. We can help prevent forest fires, though. And we can also investigate why diseases happen and help control the diseases.

People can reduce human disruptions to ecosystems in many ways. For one example, laws are made to help protect the environment and the organisms living in it from harmful chemicals, invasive species, and pollution.

Glossary

C

carnivore, n. an animal that eats other animals to meet its energy needs (25)

consumer, n. a living thing that gets energy by eating other organisms for food (4)

D

decomposer, n. an organism that breaks down dead plant and animal matter and returns nutrients to the soil (7)

disruption, n. a disturbance that interrupts a process (47)

E

ecosystem, n. all the living and nonliving things that interact in a given area (29)

F

food chain, n. a series of organisms listed in a way that shows which is a food source for another (35)

food web, n. multiple connected food chains in an ecosystem (36)

G

glucose, n. a form of sugar made by plants through the process of photosynthesis (12)

H

herbivore, n. an animal that eats plants to meet its energy needs (24)

hydroponics, n. the practice of growing plants without soil (20)

M

metabolism, n. the continuing chemical reactions in living things that release and use energy (14)

O

omnivore, n. an animal that eats both plants and other animals to meet its energy needs (27)

organism, n. a single living thing (1)

P

photosynthesis, n. the process used by producers to make glucose from sunlight, water, and carbon dioxide (12)

producer, n. a living thing that makes its own food (2)

S

scavenger, n. an animal that eats organisms that have already died (6)

sugar, n. a carbohydrate that living things break down to get energy (11)

T

transpiration, n. the release of water vapor through tiny openings in plants' leaves (18)

Core Knowledge®

CKSci™
Core Knowledge Science™

Editorial Directors
Daniel H. Franck and Richard B. Talbot

Subject Matter Expert

Christine May, PhD
Associate Professor of Biology
James Madison University
Harrisonburg, Virginia

Illustrations and Photo Credits